ARISTOTLE

Pioneering Philosopher and Founder of the Lyceum

THE LIBRARY OF GREEK PHILOSOPHERS™

ARISTOTLE

Pioneering Philosopher and Founder of the Lyceum

Mick Isle

rosen
central™

185
ISL

The Rosen Publishing Group, Inc., New York

To the sidewalk philosophers at Athens Cafe

Published in 2006 by The Rosen Publishing Group, Inc.
29 East 21st Street, New York, NY 10010

First Edition

Library of Congress Cataloging-in-Publication Data

Isle, Mick.
Aristotle: pioneering philosopher and founder of the Lyceum/ Mick Isle.
    p. cm.—(The library of Greek philosophers)
Includes bibliographical references.
ISBN 1-4042-0499-7 (library binding)
1. Aristotle. 2. Philosophers—Greece—Biography.
I. Title. II. Series.
B481.I85 2005
185--dc22

                                        2005010748

Printed in China

On the cover: Background: Circa sixteenth century (1510–1511) fresco called *School of Athens* by Raphael. Inset: Bronze bust of Aristotle from the Greek classical period (480–330 BC).

CONTENTS

INTRODUCTION

Human beings have been living in Greece for more than 7,000 years. However, it was throughout the Bronze Age (3000 BC–1200 BC) that ancient Greeks developed a highly advanced civilization. During this period, subsequent waves of maritime peoples—the Cyclads, the Minoans, and the Mycenaeans—settled on the Greek mainland and its many islands. They created new trade routes and grew wealthy through commerce. Cultural life flourished with the invention of sophisticated artistic techniques and forms of writing. New towns were founded and settled. Among them was a collection of villages that would later join together to become the city of Athens.

These cultures were suddenly stifled in the eleventh century BC when Greece was conquered by the Dorians, a people

This fresco shows human figures from the ancient city of Knossos on the isle of Crete. Crete, the largest of all the Greek islands, dates back to 3000 BC. Known as the center of Minoan civilization, Knossos was named for Minos, its famous king. Like Crete, Athens, the city that was the home of the great philosopher Aristotle, was a thriving capital.

who came from the north. For the next 200 years, Greece was trapped in a dark age, characterized by a lack of progress and wealth. Despite these hard times, Athens managed to survive and even grow. By 800 BC, the city was the leader in a new commercial, military, and cultural revival that began to take hold of Greece. Athens grew so powerful that it became a city-state, with its own government, army, laws, and traditions.

During this time, similar city-states emerged in various parts of Greece. They founded their own colonies—some as far away as Spain, Egypt, and the Ukraine—and became quite wealthy. They traded with each other and also fought wars against each other.

Aside from Athens, the other most powerful city was Sparta, which became Athens's major rival.

Between 500 BC and 400 BC, all of Greece, and Athens in particular, thrived. Attracted by the city's wealth, foreign artists and craftsmen flocked to the city. They set to work constructing magnificent palaces, temples, and theaters out of precious materials such as marble, ivory, bronze, and gold. Many other professionals, including scholars and intellectuals, migrated to Athens. Among them was a young student named Aristotle, who arrived in the still-flourishing city in 367 BC at the age of seventeen.

Aristotle and other immigrants came to take advantage of Athens's economic and educational opportunities as well as the many freedoms enjoyed by its citizens. While other Greek cities, such as Sparta, were governed by authoritarian kings who ruled with military might, in 683 BC, Athens had traded its monarchy for a constitutional government. In 500 BC, the world's first democracy was born in Athens. This "rule of the people" (*demos* was the ancient Greek word for "people" while *kratia* meant "rule") meant that all political (and most judicial) decisions were made by an assembly of the male citizens of Athens.

Athens's assembly became a place for public debate on all matters. This tradition of open discussion spread

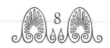

Pictured in this Venetian illuminated manuscript, Aristotle is shown as a wise man—symbolized by his long beard. Part of a manuscript dating from 1393, this portrait accompanied a text containing Latin translations of three of Aristotle's works: *Nicomachean Ethics*, *Politics*, and *Economics*.

to other public gathering places, such as the city's theaters and the main marketplace, called the agora. Democracy was evident in that citizens at every level were encouraged to express their opinions on all subjects.

Democratic Athens was ripe for the birth of many new ideas. "Philosophy" comes from the Greek words meaning "lover" (*philo*) of "wisdom" (*sophia*). In ancient Greece, philosophers were scholars who sought knowledge that would help them understand and explain the world in which they lived. They studied many subjects, ranging from physics and mathematics to biology and astronomy.

Three philosophers, in particular, took advantage of Athens's dynamic political, cultural, and intellectual scene. Socrates, his devoted student Plato, and Plato's star pupil, Aristotle, all lived, studied, and taught in Athens within an incredibly short 150-year period (470 BC–322 BC). Between them, these three men developed some of the most important and influential ideas of world civilization.

The history of Western philosophy begins with the ancient Greeks. Although great thinkers and writers existed in ancient Egyptian, Hebrew, and Arabic cultures, Greek philosophers were the first to create theories and models to explain the natural world they observed around them. Prior to Greek philosophy, most thinkers had simply reflected upon a question—such as why it rained during certain periods of the year—and then declared their conclusions as truth without any proof or evidence. Anything that couldn't be explained was said to be the result of some sort of magical action performed by invisible gods or spirits.

Socrates, Plato, and Aristotle revolutionized this new way of rational thinking about the world. Of this trio, Aristotle's impact would prove to be the most wide ranging and long lasting. Not only did Aristotle produce an enormous amount of written works, but he also brought his careful observations and reasoning to bear on a vast range of subjects. In his sixty-two years of life, Aristotle reflected upon everything from the weather, physics, and natural sciences to friendship, justice, government, and art. Armed with a critical eye and a great passion for and curiosity of life, Aristotle's ideas had a fundamental influence on the way we perceive and understand the world around us.

1 THE PHYSICIAN'S SON

Because he lived such a long time ago, many details about Aristotle's life are unknown. In particular, there is very little information about his childhood. It is certain, however, that Aristotle was born in 384 BC in Stagira, a small town in northern Greece, close to the kingdom of Macedonia, and around 175 miles (282 kilometers) from Athens. His father, Nicomachus, was a well-respected doctor who came from a long line of physicians. His mother, Phaestis, was from a wealthy family that lived on the island of Euboea, in southern Greece. Aristotle also had a brother, Arimnestus, and a sister, Arimneste, both of whom are thought to have been older than him.

Aristotle probably began school when he was around six. Most likely, he went to a neighborhood school where he learned how to read, write, and do arithmetic. Instead of a blackboard or paper, students practiced writing by scratching letters onto a wax-covered wooden block with a sharpened stick. To figure out math calculations, students counted with pebbles or a wooden tool called an abacus.

At school, boys learned how to play flutes and small harps called lyres. These were very popular instruments in ancient Greece. They also studied literature and poetry. The most famous of all Greek poems were two enormous tales by Homer: *The Iliad* and *The Odyssey*. Students had to memorize long passages—sometimes hundreds of lines—and recite them in class. During their teenage years, they practiced the art of rhetoric, or public speaking. The ability to argue and debate using sophisticated vocabulary and a dramatic style of speech was a valued trait in ancient Greek society. Those who mastered the art of rhetoric were widely respected and admired.

Outside school, Aristotle was probably tutored at home by his father. It was common practice in ancient Greece for doctors to teach their sons about science and medicine. As a young boy, Aristotle probably learned a fair bit about human anatomy and diseases by observing Nicomachus at work. He likely accompanied his father when he went searching

This map shows the various states of Greece during the time of the Peloponnesian War (477 BC–404 BC). The war, which was fought between Athens and Sparta, was the second war between these two powerful city-states.

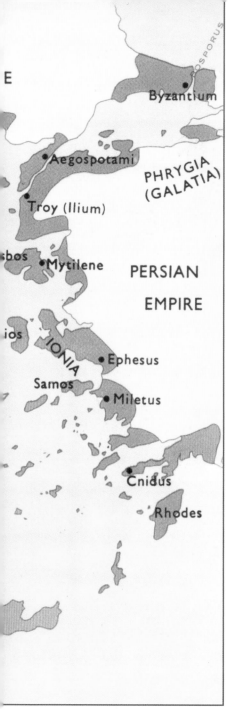

for medicinal plants and herbs. These were used as remedies for common ailments such as stomachaches and fevers. Such early experiences might help account for Aristotle's later interest in natural sciences—biology, botany, and zoology. In ancient Greece, the profession of physician was passed down directly from father to son. It was thus probable that Nicomachus was training Aristotle to be a doctor.

When Aristotle was still very young, King Amyntas II of Macedonia hired Nicomachus to be his personal physician. The men in Aristotle's family had a long tradition of serving as physicians to Macedonian kings. At the Macedonian royal court, Aristotle made friends with the king's youngest son, Philip. The two boys were roughly the same age.

When Aristotle was ten years old, his father died. His mother

Homer

Considered one of the great poets of all times, it is believed that Homer lived in the eighth century BC. Almost nothing is known about his life aside from the fact that he was blind. In fact, some scholars wonder if he really existed or if he was a legend. At the time Homer lived, poetry was spoken instead of written. Homer would have composed and memorized *The Iliad* and *The Odyssey* and then traveled throughout Greece reciting them to audiences. Over time, these poems became the two most important works in ancient Greek culture. They were recited and memorized by generations of Greeks.

Aside from their literary and historic value, these poems were also used as guides for moral behavior. The heroes' decisions and actions provided young Greeks with many lessons about honor and friendship, courage and justice. Many Greek gods and goddesses, such as Apollo, Athena, and Aphrodite, appeared as characters in both poems, thus revealing the importance of religion in Greek life.

The Iliad tells the tale of the ten-year Trojan War fought between the Greeks and the Trojans, whose legendary city is situated in present-day Turkey. The war broke out after Prince Paris of Troy kidnapped the beautiful Helen, wife of the powerful Greek king, Menelaus. Homer's epic poem features brutally realistic battle scenes between heroic characters. These include Agamemnon, the proud leader of the Greek forces and Menelaus's brother, and the brave but doomed King Hector of Troy. Most famous of all was Achilles, the invincible Greek warrior whose only weak spot was his heel. Both dramatic and tragic, *The Iliad* deals with human themes such as pride and courage, honor, and vanity.

The Odyssey is a wonderful adventure story that describes the Greek soldier Odysseus's journey home after the Trojan War. This journey (by land and by sea) takes him ten years. To be reunited with his wife and son, the hero relies on his intelligence as well as sly trickery to overcome monsters, storms, the anger of the gods, and many other obstacles. Aside from inventing one of the world's most memorable heroes, Homer's tale led to "odyssey" becoming an English word. It is used to describe a great adventurous journey or quest.

died shortly thereafter. Suddenly an orphan, young Aristotle was taken in and raised by a close friend of his father's, Proxenus, who lived in the city of Atarneus. Leaving behind his medical apprenticeship, Aristotle (who was a teenager at the time) spent much of his time studying poetry and rhetoric.

Shortly after Aristotle's parents' deaths, King Amyntas died, too. As a result of the king's death, Macedonia experienced a period of upheaval. Armed political rebellions lasted for several years. Proxenus must have felt that amid this unstable environment,

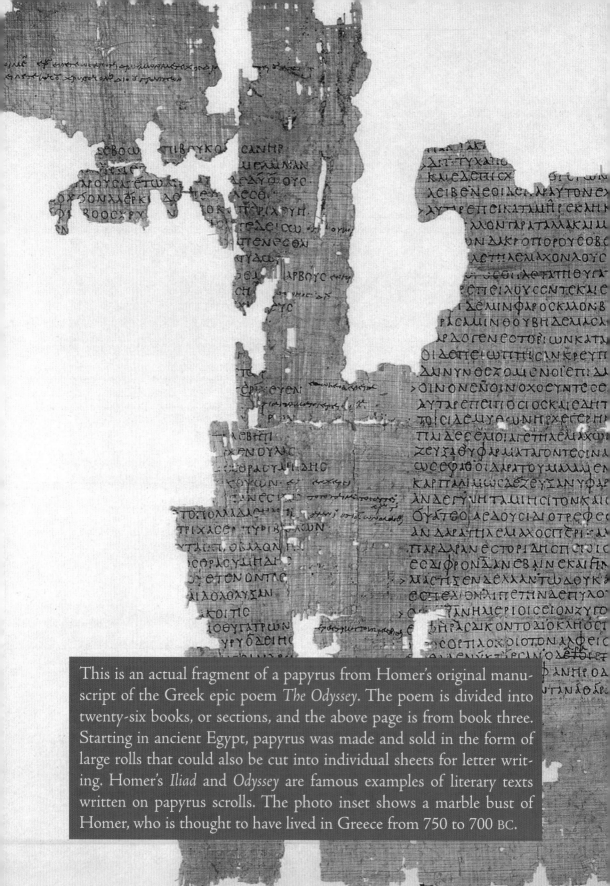

This is an actual fragment of a papyrus from Homer's original manuscript of the Greek epic poem *The Odyssey*. The poem is divided into twenty-six books, or sections, and the above page is from book three. Starting in ancient Egypt, papyrus was made and sold in the form of large rolls that could also be cut into individual sheets for letter writing. Homer's *Iliad* and *Odyssey* are famous examples of literary texts written on papyrus scrolls. The photo inset shows a marble bust of Homer, who is thought to have lived in Greece from 750 to 700 BC.

Aristotle would have a difficult time securing his future. As a consequence, when he was seventeen, Aristotle was sent to continue his studies in the great city of Athens.

ATHENS

The site upon which the city of Athens was built had been inhabited since prehistoric times. Surrounded by protective mountains, its acropolis—the Greek word for "high city"—provided sweeping views of the surrounding plains and sea. It was for strategic purposes

A young and thoughtful Aristotle is depicted in this marble sculpture from the nineteenth century. Aside from being known as a great philosopher, Aristotle was also a noted scientist. Of particular interest was his writings on biology. He was especially intrigued with the study of aquatic life such as dolphins, torpedo fish, and viviparous sharks (meaning that they do not lay eggs).

What Was Aristotle Like?

A Greek historian named Diogenes Laertius, who lived in the third century AD (500 years after Aristotle), was the first to write a biography about the major Greek philosophers. Diogenes describes Aristotle as a somewhat elegant man who stood out in a crowd due to his clothing and jewelry and the way he cut his hair. He apparently had very thin legs and spoke with a lisp. According to Diogenes, Aristotle was a kind man who was generous to his family and friends. Although he had a serious nature, he had a good sense of humor and was known to joke with his colleagues and students.

that the Mycenaeans had decided to build a fortified settlement on the rocky acropolis. Over time, this settlement grew into a city called Athinai. Its name honored the city's protectress: Athena, the Greek goddess of wisdom.

Crowning the acropolis was the Parthenon, an impressive temple devoted to Athena. It was the city's most important religious monument. Inside the temple was a forty-foot (twelve-meter) statue of Athena cast in gold and ivory. At the bottom of the acropolis was the Theater of Dionysus, built in honor

Above is a reconstruction of the Athena Parthenos. This gigantic and regal statue of the goddess Athena originally measured close to 40 feet (12 m). It is one of the works of Athenian sculptor Phidias, who was the artistic director of the construction of the Parthenon. The original statue dates from 438 BC. Athena is shown wearing a helmet and holding Nike (the goddess of victory) in her right hand. By her side are a decorated shield and a serpent.

of the Greek god of wine and celebration. Here, audiences watched plays or musical performances while sitting on a half circle of stone benches built into the hillside (known as an amphitheater). At the time, drama festivals were very popular. They were paid for with city taxes. Wealthy Athenians also helped

In ancient Greece, many of the major city-states were constructed around an acropolis, similar to this famous one in Athens. Meaning "high city," these fortifications were sought out by citizens seeking safety in times of war and enemy invasions. Because the Acropolis was a peaceful refuge, many of the most sacred buildings in Greek architecture were constructed there. The main architect of the Acropolis in Athens was a colleague of Phidias (creator of the Athena Parthenos) named Mnesicles.

subsidize performers' fees. Aristocratic families considered it an honor to donate money to the arts.

Between the sixth and fifth centuries BC, Athens became a renowned center of literature and the arts. Many of ancient Greece's greatest playwrights and poets were living in Athens. Writers such as Aeschylus, Aristophanes, Euripides, Simonides, and Sophocles (author of the play *Oedipus the King*) produced some of the most powerful works in Western literature.

Although in the fifth century BC Athens had a population of roughly 320,000 people, only around 50,000 were considered Athenian citizens with full rights (such as the right to vote and participate in public life). Almost a third of Athenian society was made up of slaves. Men and women were born into slavery or became slaves after being captured in wars between Athens and other city-states or kingdoms. Although slaves had to do the most difficult work, in Athens, they were generally treated much better and enjoyed more freedoms than slaves in other Greek cities.

Some received wages with which they could eventually buy their freedom. Others, who worked in the homes of the wealthy, were treated like members of the family. In fact, foreigners criticized Athens because they said it was difficult to tell the difference between slaves and free citizens. Outside Athens, it was often believed that slaves were inferior beings who didn't deserve to be treated like humans.

Women also did not have rights as citizens. They could not vote, walk in the streets, or even take part in theatrical productions (female roles were played by males). Because they were expected to grow up and become wives and mothers, girls didn't go to school. Instead, they stayed at home where their mothers taught them how to weave fabric, sew clothing, and cook. These tasks were necessary since most girls would wed and start to raise families by the age of fifteen or sixteen.

Metics, the name given to men from other cities who immigrated to Athens, were also denied the political rights of Athenian citizens. Although they were free, they could not participate in political assemblies, nor could they vote. Aristotle, too, was considered a metic because he was foreign-born.

Two Great Masters

When he arrived in Athens, Aristotle went to study at a school known as the Academy. Though it had only been in existence for twenty years, the Academy was a distinguished center of learning. This was due to the reputation of its founder, director, and principal teacher—the great philosopher Plato.

PHILOSOPHY

Ancient Greek philosophers transformed Western thinking by asking fundamental questions and seeking answers based on logical reasoning and scientific observation. Attempting to understand the world around them, these philosophers considered four major questions:

> 1. Where do things (living and nonliving) come from?

2. What are they made of?
3. How does one explain so many different things in nature?
4. How can one describe all of these things?

The rational methods they used to answer these questions laid the foundations for modern philosophy and science. One of the first and greatest of the ancient Greek philosophers was a man named Socrates. Socrates' most important contribution to Western thought was his method of inquiry, or asking questions.

SOCRATES

An Athenian citizen, Socrates was born in 469 BC. His father was a stonemason and his mother was a midwife. As an adult, Socrates compared his role as a philosopher to that of a midwife. However, in this analogy, instead of helping give birth to a baby, he delivered the truth.

Socrates was growing up while Athens was at the height of its power and influence as a cultural and intellectual center. As a young man, he spent much time in the streets of Athens. It was here that the great thinkers and artists of the day debated (in public) their advanced ideas. Even once he was an adult

This fresco of Socrates was discovered in Ephesus, Turkey. The Socratic method of philosophical inquiry consisted of continual questioning of a person until, through inevitable contradictions, the person's ideas were proved wrong. This form of questioning was called *elenchus* by Socrates and Plato. Plato is thought to have been the most accurate scholar to convey Socrates' philosophical ideas in writing. Socrates himself did not write down any of his theories.

and was married, Socrates continued to spend lots of time in Athens's lively marketplaces or at banquets in private homes. In these situations, intellectual debates were carried on for hours at a time. His wife was apparently angered by his frequent absences from home. However, Socrates' socializing gave him the opportunity to indulge in his favorite intellectual activity: questioning people about what they knew—and didn't.

A true "lover of wisdom," Socrates became obsessed with discovering truths about the world. Even though he was considered by many to be the wisest man in Athens, Socrates believed he was quite ignorant about many subjects. In fact, he argued that

it was his ignorance that made him wise. By admitting he lacked knowledge about a subject, he would be forced to ask questions if he wanted to understand it better. By repeatedly questioning many people, he would gradually get closer to the truth about something. Socrates never accepted a simple yes or no answer. Instead, he would ask open-ended questions that would invite people to explain and justify their opinions. Often, he wouldn't arrive at a final conclusion about a subject. However, the conversations themselves were important since they revealed that people didn't always know what they thought they did. Socrates believed that discovering the fact that our knowledge has limits was what made us want to learn more. This belief was summed up in one of Socrates' most famous quotes:

The unexamined life isn't worth living.

Socrates particularly enjoyed entering into debates with a group of thinkers and teachers of rhetoric known as the Sophists (givers of wisdom). In Athens, it was fashionable for wealthy Athenians, particularly politicians, to hire the Sophists to teach them how to speak and debate effectively. Socrates openly criticized the Sophists, condemning the fact that they charged money to share views that were based on unexamined assumptions. His constant debates with the Sophists became so well known that they inspired a famous play. *The Clouds* was a comedy written by Aristophanes, one of Athens's most reputed dramatists. The play made fun of Socrates and his long-winded inquiries.

During this period, Athens was increasingly threatened by its longtime rival, Sparta. Relations between the two city-states deteriorated until fighting broke out in 458 BC. Over the next fifty years, Athens and Sparta fought several wars, which finally ended with an Athenian defeat in 404 BC. Athens lost its renowned naval fleet and its overseas colonies. The Spartans also replaced Athens's democratic assembly with a strict government ruled by the Thirty Tyrants. (In ancient times a tyrant was a leader who ruled with absolute power.) These Tyrants exiled and killed many of their political enemies and reduced the number of citizens from approximately 30,000 to only 3,000 of their loyal supporters. Several of the Tyrants were Socrates' former students. As a result, he was chosen to be one of these select citizens. However, when Socrates spoke out against the unjust arrest of an important foreign resident, he made enemies in the new government.

Soon after, Sparta lost control of its conquests. As a result, Athens regained much of its economic force and its democratic government. Even though he had stood up for what he believed in, Socrates' association with the Thirty Tyrants made him an enemy of democracy in the eyes of the new Athenian government. Furthermore, some Athenians felt his beliefs—such as his famous phrase "the majority is always wrong"—to be antidemocratic.

Socrates' Apology

In 399 BC, the Athenian court of justice accused Socrates of corrupting the city's youth. Socrates, who was seventy at the time, argued that his teaching young Athenians to question life had, in fact, been very positive. In his famous work *Apology*, Socrates' most brilliant pupil, Plato, recorded the self-defense that Socrates gave to the jury at his trial:

To put it bluntly I've been assigned to this city as if to a large horse which is inclined to be lazy and is in need of some great stinging fly and all day long I'll never cease to settle here, there, everywhere, rousing [stirring to action] and reproving [criticizing] every one of you.

Angered by the directness of this statement, the jury found Socrates guilty of the crimes with which he was charged. In keeping with Athenian tradition, the accuser and the accused were asked to propose a penalty. The accuser proposed death, while Socrates declared that he should receive the city's highest

In this drawing, Socrates (center) is drinking a cup of poisonous hemlock. Plato's famous work *Apology* describes Socrates' defense at his trial. In fact, the English word "apology" is derived from the Greek word for "a speech in defense." Hemlock is an herb that grows twice a year. The leaves make one nauseous and ultimately lead to a coma and then death.

honors. These were usually reserved for Olympic athletes. Enraged by what they viewed as excessive pride, the jury gave him the extreme punishment the accuser had requested.

Socrates' last days were spent in jail, where he was visited by many friends and students. He refused to take part in friends' plans to help him escape from prison and faced his death without fear. As friends wept openly, Socrates drank the cup of poisonous hemlock that killed him.

PLATO

One of Socrates' most devoted young students was Plato. Plato's real name was Aristocles. He was born in 427 BC to a wealthy Athenian family. The nickname Plato was acquired during his adolescence when he practiced the popular sport of wrestling. The Greek word for "broad," the name Plato likely referred to young Aristocles' muscular physique.

At the age of twenty, Plato began studying with Socrates. Like other teachers, Socrates held classes outdoors in the streets and marketplaces of Athens, where students would gather around and listen to him. Socrates was a great influence on young Plato. When Socrates was sentenced to death, Plato attended his trial. Many of Plato's earliest writings record his memories of his teacher, including Socrates' trial and death.

Both of these events had a strong impact on Plato. He felt that Socrates had been the victim of a great injustice. He was so angered by the role of Athens's democratic government in Socrates' death that he left the city after the philosopher's execution. Much of Plato's later writings on politics and ethics reflected his search for an ideal society where such injustices wouldn't occur. In fact, in his most renowned work, *The Republic* (written in his later years, circa 360 BC), Plato proposes a form of government ruled by philosophers. His most famous written works were composed in the form of dialogues between two or more speakers with different points of view. They were based on the long question and answer sessions that Socrates had used as his method of inquiry. Often, the main character in these written debates was Socrates himself. As such, many of Socrates' ideas were faithfully recorded.

After Socrates' death, Plato spent the next twelve years traveling throughout Greece, Egypt, Italy, and Sicily. Aside from many adventures (according to

This is a copper engraving of the Greek philosopher Plato. The school Plato opened, the Academy (or Academia), was initially a public garden situated in the Athenian suburbs. The name "Academia" comes from Akademos, who had left the grove to the citizens of Athens so they would have a peaceful green space where they could practice gymnastics.

rumors, he was captured by pirates and sold as a slave) he learned a great deal. When he finally returned to Athens, he decided to continue Socrates' legacy as a teacher. However, instead of lecturing in the streets, he decided to buy a plot of land and open

This illuminated manuscript shows Plato (*left*) and Socrates (*right*). Most of what is known about Socrates comes from Plato's dialogues (close to thirty) as well as four short works by Socrates' friend Xenophan. The dialogues feature Socrates as the main speaker. In the above image, Socrates is shown writing down ideas. However, he is not known to have written down anything. Nearly all of Plato's writings (the student was in fact forty years younger than his mentor) date from after the trial and death of Socrates.

up a permanent school. This would become the first university in the Western world.

The land Plato purchased, an olive grove, had once belonged to an Athenian named Akademos. In his honor, Plato called his school the Academy (which, in turn, became the origin of the English word "academics"). Even though there were buildings where students could sleep and eat, classes were held outdoors beneath the trees.

Plato's aim was to teach numerous subjects ranging from politics and philosophy to mathematics and medicine. Attracted by Plato's fame and the school's mission, students from all over Greece came to study at the Academy. No examinations or diplomas were given. Students studied simply because they wanted to acquire knowledge.

As a philosopher, Plato wrote on subjects as varied as science, mathematics, justice, government, love, and the notion of the human soul. He was also concerned with the pursuit of virtue in politics and art, and among human beings. In *The Republic*, he described his ideal city-state in which all citizens have a specific job (tailor, farmer, banker, wife, etc.) allowing them to contribute to the wealth, success, and harmony of society. He also examined different types of government, such as monarchy and democracy, in an

Platonism

One of Plato's most important contributions to philosophy was the way he viewed reality. Plato believed that all things in the world were present in two forms. Ideal forms can be understood but cannot be detected by human senses. (For instance, one can understand the idea of air, although air cannot be seen, heard, or touched.) In contrast, perceptual, or objective forms (for example, water), can be perceived by the human senses. Plato demonstrated this notion using the example of a carpenter who is about to make a chair. Because of his knowledge, in his mind, the carpenter has an image of an ideal chair he plans to make. However, this imagined chair is never the same as the real, physical chair he ends up constructing. Furthermore, if the carpenter makes fifty chairs, none will be the same owing to the differences in wood, the tools used, and the care taken by the carpenter. Therefore, chairs, like all objects, exist in two forms: the perfect or ideal chair and the real chairs that carpenters actually make that can be sat upon.

Plato viewed the entire physical world in this manner. For instance, the idea of a dog conjured up in someone's head is different from the various types of dogs that people own as pets. This distinction led Plato to believe that the world was created by a perfect craftsman known as God. Inspired by perfect forms, this creator made everything in the world as copies or images of them. This vision of the world came to be known as Platonism.

attempt to determine which one was the most virtuous. Ultimately, he proposed a state ruled by wise and well-educated "philosopher-kings." As described in *The Republic*, these were "men . . . perfected by years and education." Having viewed the way the Athenian assembly had turned on his mentor, Socrates, he was very critical of democracy.

ARISTOTLE THE STUDENT

By the time Aristotle began studying at the Academy, Plato was already considered one of Greece's most

This tile from the Santa Maria del Fiore Church in Florence, Italy, depicts Aristotle in deep philosophical discussion with Plato. Plato is perhaps best known for his writings in *The Republic*. Aristotle was only eighteen years old when he started out at the Academy as a student of Plato's. Aristotle, who later would open his own school, the Lyceum, was often referred to as a polymath, meaning that he had in-depth knowledge on a vast array of subjects.

important philosophers. Aristotle was so eager to learn that his colleagues often called him Anagnostes, the Greek word for "the reader." Soon, Plato was referring to his bright student as "the intelligence of the school."

It wasn't long before Aristotle himself began teaching at the Academy. Aristotle greatly admired Plato, and the two had a close relationship. However, as time went by, Aristotle began to question some of Plato's views and develop a philosophy of his own.

3 THE NATURAL SCIENTIST

Aristotle remained at Plato's Academy for almost twenty years. Over time, his rejection of many of Plato's ideas caused his teacher to say the following, "Aristotle spurns [rejects] me as colts kick out the mother who bore them." Nevertheless, while the two men had conflicting ideas on many subjects, they had a great deal of admiration for each other.

PLATO VS. ARISTOTLE

The major conflict between Plato and Aristotle stemmed from Plato's beliefs in an ideal world that was a model of perfection and couldn't be detected by the senses. Aristotle believed in a physical world whose laws could be observed, measured, and investigated. He disagreed

This famous fresco by the Italian artist Raphael, called *The School of Athens*, shows Plato (wearing orange and blue, with a long beard) and Aristotle (to his left), as well as many other important philosophers such as Socrates and Xenophanes at the Lyceum.

with the notion of a divine creator who made the universe out of unformed materials. Instead, Aristotle put forth the idea of a natural world with its own laws, order, and logic, which had been set into motion but not created by God. For instance, if one plants an acorn, one knows it will grow into an oak tree and not a birch tree.

While Plato divided the world into the ideal and the real, Aristotle saw things as "potential beings" and "actual beings." An acorn, for instance, has the potential to be an oak tree. An oak tree has the potential of becoming a chair. At any given time, everything in the world possesses both states—the form it is actually in (a tree) and the many possible forms it can become (a chair, a table, firewood, etc.).

This belief led Aristotle to formulate the argument that

The School of Athens

In 1510, the great Italian Renaissance painter Raphael created a magnificent mural called *The School of Athens* for the pope's palace at the Vatican. The center of this work shows a robust Aristotle walking next to a bald, white-bearded Plato. The palm of Aristotle's right hand, which is positioned facing downward, symbolizes the importance of the earth and the perceptible natural world. Beside him, Plato walks with his index finger pointing toward the heavens. This stance represents his belief in the power of thought and abstract ideals. By positioning the two philosophers side by side, Raphael was suggesting that the future of philosophy was in unifying both of these ancient ways of thinking.

everything on Earth was in a constant state of fluctuation. Seasons change as do climatic conditions. Plants, animals, and humans are born, grow, decay, and die. The four essential elements—air, fire, earth, and water—were responsible for these shifts. Aristotle believed that all matter consisted of these four elements in their pure form or combined.

Each of these elements had its own specific properties. Air and fire, for instance were light, while earth and water were heavy. Air, however, was hot and wet,

This illustration from Aristotle's treatise, *Physics* shows a philosopher holding a globe that contains the four elements—earth, air, fire, and water. The first line in chapter one of book 2 of *Physics* reads as follows: "Of things that exist, some exist by nature, some from other causes. By nature the animals and their parts exist, and the plants and the simple bodies [earth, fire, air, water]—for we say that these and the like exist by nature. . . ."

while fire was hot and dry. Similarly, while earth was cold and dry, water was cold and wet. The properties that characterized these elements offered logical explanations for all matter that existed on Earth. For instance, when dropped, rocks fall downward (toward Earth) because they are made of the earth itself and are heavy. The light and dry flames of a fire shoot upward (toward the fiery gases that exist above the air). As well, substances could change their outer form and mix with other elements. For example, water could become steam, rain, or a river. Earth (mixed with water) could transform into clay, which in turn (when heated by fire) could become a ceramic vessel. However, despite these transformations in form, their essential matter remained intact. For example, both snow and vapor are two different forms of water.

ASSOS

In 347 BC, Plato died in his sleep. He was eighty years old. Shortly after, thirty-seven-year-old Aristotle decided to leave the Academy and Athens. Aristotle was by far the most brilliant teacher at the Academy. However, on his deathbed, Plato had chosen his nephew, an undistinguished scholar, to replace him as director of the school. This snub might have been a reason for Aristotle's departure. Nonetheless, Aristotle himself claimed to be unhappy with the Academy's growing emphasis on mathematics while natural sciences (his favorite subject) were being ignored.

Around the same time, tensions were growing between Athens and Macedonia. Under the rule of King Amyntas's youngest son, Philip, Macedonia's power and influence had been growing. An ambitious leader, Philip had conquered much of northern Greece, including Aristotle's birthplace, Stagira. Athenians felt increasingly threatened by Philip's aggressive posture, and hostilities ran high. As a non-citizen with ties to the Macedonian court, Aristotle might have felt uncomfortable remaining in the city where he was considered by some Athenians to be pro-Macedonian.

As a result of all these factors, Aristotle set off on a journey throughout Greece and Asia Minor (present-day Turkey). In Asia Minor, he visited the coastal city of Assos, where he was welcomed by King Hermias. Hermias, an old friend and fellow student of Aristotle's at the Academy, had started out very poor in life before rising to power. With the help of the neighboring king of Persia—King Artaxerxes—he succeeded in seizing the throne of Assos. Under his rule, Assos had developed into an important intellectual and cultural center and Hermias encouraged his scholarly friend to settle there and share his knowledge. Ultimately, Aristotle became director of a school of philosophy similar to the Academy. He then married Hermias's niece, Pythias, who was around eighteen at the time. Together, they had a daughter named Pythias.

For the next few years, Aristotle and his new family lived in tranquility. However, during this time, Hermias began to become friendly with Philip of Macedonia. King Artaxerxes (who had helped keep Hermias in power) was not pleased with this new alliance. In 344 BC, he invited Hermias to Persia. Instead of a friendly visit, Hermias was taken prisoner and tortured. Soon after, he was crucified. Aristotle was devastated. Shortly after, he moved to Lesbos—a nearby island in the Aegean Sea—because he felt it was no longer safe for his family to remain in Assos.

On Lesbos, Aristotle became close friends with a young scholar named Theophrastus. Both men were fascinated by the study of the natural world. Theophrastus was interested in plant life. Meanwhile, Aristotle began to collect and study the sea creatures that lived in the warm Aegean waters. He soon extended his study of sea animals to all living creatures.

On Lesbos, students, other teachers, and local fishermen helped him collect new specimens. Travelers told him stories about animals they had encountered on their voyages. These tales, along with his own observations, helped him create detailed descriptions of many living creatures. At the time, this study of animals and their behavior was unheard of. Serious philosophers were supposed to be concerned with more "scientific" subjects, such as mathematics, ethics, and astronomy. Aristotle defended his passion by declaring that animals (aside from being just as fascinating) were easier to study than faraway stars.

ARISTOTLE AND ZOOLOGY

Aristotle's study of living creatures led him to invent the science known as zoology. Zoology refers to the classification and study of animals. Aristotle was the first person to create a system of classifying animals according to their characteristics and habits. Over time, he gave names to and described more than 500 types of animals.

Frequently, Aristotle dissected the animals, cutting them open in order to study their internal organs, such as heart, brain, and liver. The notes he took on animals included observations of their daily habits and behavior—how they hunted, mated, gave birth, and related to other creatures. Some of his descriptions

Classifying Animals

Once he had observed and gathered information about creatures, Aristotle was able to divide them into types or species. The first major distinction he made was between "bloodless" animals—those without vertebrae, or backbones—and "blooded" animals with backbones. These categories were then further subdivided as follows:

"Bloodless" Animals (Invertebrates)	"Blooded" Animals (Vertebrates)
• Animals with soft exteriors (octopus, squid) • Animals with armor-like hard exteriors that can be smashed (crabs, lobsters) • Animals with hard shell-like exteriors that must be hammered open (oysters, snails) • Insects	• Human beings • Birds • Four-footed animals that give birth to offspring (horses, dogs) • Four-footed animals that lay eggs (lizards) • Fish that give birth to offspring (whales, dolphins) • Fish that lay eggs (tuna, salmon)

Aristotle was aware that these broad categories were not exact. For instance, he knew that while they lived in the sea and gave birth to their young in the water, whales and dolphins were technically mammals and not fish.

Aside from his philosophical writings, Aristotle became renowned for his early work in biology, in particular, with reference to the classification of animals. Pictured in this fresco in the Assemblée Nationale in Paris, France, Aristotle is describing the animals that were sent to him by Alexander the Great. Ahead of his time, many of Aristotle's accurate deductions about animals remained the scientific standard in biology for centuries to come. He wrote about Earth sciences in a treatise called *Meteorology*.

(included in his published works *The History of Animals* [circa 350 BC] and *On the Parts of Animals* [circa 350 BC]) were very lively. For example, he wrote that elephants' trunks produced a noise like a hoarse trumpet and compared hyenas' cries to the noise of a man throwing up. He praised the octopus for its tidy housekeeping habits.

Aristotle also showed interest in human anatomy. Unfortunately, religious rules prohibited the dissection of humans. This made studying the human body a complicated task. However, based on the animals he dissected, Aristotle made some conclusions about human beings. Over time, some of these turned out to

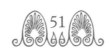

be inaccurate. He believed, for example, that the heart was the center of all intelligence, while the brain functioned as a type of air conditioner to the heart, cooling the blood as it circulated throughout the body.

In exploring how an animal got along with other animals (or didn't), adapted to the climate, and searched for food, water, and shelter, Aristotle ended up making many observations about the animal's environment. In doing so, he was the first to link the study of living things to their natural habitats. This science later became known as ecology.

ALEXANDER THE GREAT

After a year or two in Lesbos, Aristotle received an invitation from King Philip II of Macedonia. The king wanted the son of his father's former physician to come to his court at Pella and tutor his thirteen-year-old son, Alexander. Aristotle accepted the offer. Upon his arrival, he was pleased to discover that his new student was an exceptionally bright and curious young man.

Aristotle and Alexander quickly formed a close bond. Aside from natural history, Aristotle taught the young prince a great deal about politics, philosophy, and ethics—all of which were important subjects

On the left, a young Alexander the Great is seen being taught by Aristotle (*seated at far left*). On the right, he is being instructed by other teachers. In section six of his book *Life of Alexander*, Plutarch of Chaeronea mentions the location where Alexander's father suggested that Aristotle teach his son. "As a place for the pursuit of their studies and exercise, he assigned the temple of the Nymphs, near Mieza, where, to this very day, they show you Aristotle's stone seats, and the shady walks which he was wont to frequent."

for a future king. He also taught him poetry, including the works of Homer. Alexander was particularly impressed by the action-filled *Iliad*. He memorized most of the 16,000 lines of this epic poem.

When Alexander turned sixteen, Philip believed it was time for his son to learn about warfare. In order to gain military experience, Alexander joined his father's army. At the age of seventeen, the young prince led a successful attack on the armies of Athens and another city-state called Thebes. He was well on his way to proving himself as an intelligent and fearless warrior and military commander.

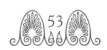

Bucephalus

Aside from being intelligent, young Alexander was also very brave. Some time before Aristotle's arrival in Macedonia, King Philip planned to buy a beautiful horse for his son. However, the horse was so wild that none of the stable hands could mount it. Philip was ready to change his mind when Alexander spoke up and bragged that he would be able to ride the horse. He was so sure of himself that Philip agreed to let him try. The king promised that if Alexander succeeded in riding it, the horse would be his. However, if he didn't succeed, Alexander would have to pay his father the price of the horse—the equivalent of more than $1,000.

Alexander was sure he would win his father's bet. He had watched the stable hands trying to mount the horse. He noticed that the horse bucked and reared because it was scared by its own shadow. Accordingly, before mounting the horse, Alexander led it into a position directly facing the sun. With its shadow behind it, the animal was calm and allowed Alexander to ride him. King Philip was so proud of his son that he cried tears of joy. In his *Life of Alexander* (circa AD 100), the Greek historian Plutarch (circa AD 45–125) said the king cried, "O my son, look thee out a kingdom equal to and worthy of thyself, for Macedonia is too little for thee."

Philip's words would prove to be prophetic. Meanwhile, Alexander named his new horse Bucephalus. From then on, Bucephalus became the young prince's closest companion.

Four years later, in 336 BC, Philip was murdered and Alexander became Macedonia's new king as well as commander in chief of its impressive army. His military experience had left Alexander eager to

The title of this French illuminated manuscript is "How Alexander the Great Mounted Bucephalus." Once Alexander figured out that the beautiful black stallion was afraid of his own shadow, man and animal became inseparable. In fact, Alexander rode Bucephalus during all of his battles. After Bucephalus died during a battle in India in 327 BC, Alexander was so distraught that he named a city in India in his honor.

continue his father's goal of conquering other lands. However, his ambitions were such that he vowed to keep fighting until he had conquered the entire known world.

Waging battle after battle, he led his troops east through Asia. Accompanying him was his constant companion, Bucephalus, and a copy of *The Iliad*, which he placed under his pillow every night. In fact, *The Iliad* was never far from the great warrior's thoughts. Early in his campaign, Alexander had insisted upon visiting the legendary city of Troy. With a few close friends, he sought out the grave of the Greek hero Achilles. According to legend, Alexander uncovered old pieces of armor from the Trojan War. Hoping they would bring him luck, he wore them in battle.

Aristotle's nephew, Callisthenes, was asked to travel with the troops and keep a journal of Alexander's adventures. He was only one of many non-soldiers who accompanied Alexander and his troops. Others included poets who were hired to compose glorious battle epics, entertain tired soldiers with songs, and recite poetry. Engineers, philosophers, geographers, and natural scientists also came along to study the different cultures, technologies, traditions, and plant and animal life of the countries conquered.

During his campaign, Alexander never forgot his former tutor. He ordered that Aristotle's hometown of Stagira (which had been severely damaged in a fire) be rebuilt. When he conquered Lesbos, where Aristotle's friend Theophrastus lived, he prohibited his soldiers from looting homes and businesses. He also made sure that the botanists and biologists who accompanied him sent interesting plant and animal specimens back to Aristotle.

Alexander's military campaigns took him all the way to India. Along the way, he conquered many great cities, including Herat (in present-day Afghanistan) and Samarqand (in present-day Uzbekistan). He also founded several new ones. One of the most important was Alexandria, in Egypt, which he named after himself. Strategically situated at the point where the Nile River joins the Mediterranean Sea, Alexandria soon developed into one of the ancient world's major cultural, intellectual, and commercial centers.

RETURN TO ATHENS

Aristotle had not accompanied Alexander on his conquests. After spending some time in Pella and then in Stagira, in 335 BC, Aristotle decided to go back to Athens. His return marked the first time he had been

This tapestry depicts a scene from the Battle of Issus, where Alexander the Great won a battle over Darius III, the last leader of the Persian Empire. The death of Darius meant that after more than two centuries, the Achaemenid dynasty had come to a decisive end. Nonetheless, Alexander gave Darius a magnificent funeral after he was killed in 330 BC.

to the city in twelve years. At age fifty, he dreamed of starting his own school—one similar to the Academy—where he could share his knowledge with young students.

At this time, Athens, which was under Macedonian rule, was governed by Alexander. Since Aristotle was not a citizen of Athens, he couldn't buy land for his school. However, with the aid of Macedonian officials, he was able to rent some land outside the city walls. A temple built to honor the god Apollo Lyceus was situated on the land. Because of this, Aristotle's school came to be called the Lyceum.

4 THE LYCEUM

Aristotle ran the Lyceum differently from the way Plato had run the Academy. While Plato had encouraged discussions and dialogues between students and teachers, Aristotle preferred to focus on lectures and scientific research. According to historical accounts, Aristotle himself was a brilliant and articulate teacher.

He often gave his lectures while strolling up and down the path that led to the temple of Apollo Lyceus. His students were forced to follow closely behind if they wanted to hear his lessons in their entirety. They were subsequently called the Peripatetics— Greek for "walkabouts" or "wanderers." The Lyceum itself became known as the Peripatetic School.

Archaeologists believe that the above ruins are what is left of Aristotle's Lyceum. This aerial view was photographed when archaeologists were on a dig at the site of a new modern art museum in Athens.

A SCHOLARLY LIFE

Aristotle usually taught more advanced students in the morning. Afternoons were reserved for lectures for the general public. Ultimately, Aristotle spent thirteen years at the Lyceum. It was during this time that he produced most of his written pieces. Many of his lecture notes were collected and later published. Aristotle also wrote dialogues based on debates he had with his students. Inspired by Plato's dialogues, these works were written in a more common, everyday language than his other classics, which tended to be more dense and technical.

Aristotle had always been a great collector of books. When he founded the Lyceum, he created the first great library in Greece. His private collection was enriched by the numerous books that Alexander sent to him from his travels. In fact, Aristotle's library at the Lyceum was the inspiration for the famed library of Alexandria. As well, with the many animal and plant specimens that Alexander sent from faraway lands, Aristotle was able to create an important museum of natural history.

These resources helped Aristotle attract an impressive array of scholars to the Lyceum. Here, they taught and conducted research. Among them was his

This colored woodcut illustrates Aristotle *(far left)* with his students at the Lyceum. In 1997, after the Lyceum was unearthed by archaeologists, Evangelos Venizelos, the minister of culture of Greece came forth to attest to the certainty of the archaeologists' find. He stated, "There is no doubt whatsoever that this is the school where Aristotle taught."

old friend from Lesbos, Theophrastus. At the Lyceum, students could learn about every subject imaginable at the time. In the first century BC, the famous Roman orator Cicero (106 BC–43 BC) compared the Lyceum to a factory that produced professionals of every kind: diplomats, military commanders, doctors, engineers, poets, and even musicians.

One of Aristotle's most important contributions at the Lyceum was the development of an early version

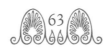

of the scientific method. Scientific method refers to the process by which scientists try to construct an accurate representation of the world. Based on rational thought, Aristotle developed this scientific method, which could be used to find answers to many types of questions. It not only influenced all teaching and research at the Lyceum, but the scientific method also revolutionized Western thinking forever.

LOGIC

Aristotle claimed that when studying any problem, the first step was to research all available information. It was not enough to simply read this information. One had to examine it with a critical eye to judge if it made sense. Any doubtful information or faulty conclusions needed to be questioned and reexamined. After coming up with one's own solution to the problem, a good researcher needed to seek evidence that would support his or her point of view. This in turn could (and should) be questioned by other scholars. By following such a rational system of investigation, human knowledge of the world could constantly progress, while flawed conclusions and beliefs could be discarded.

This scientific reasoning—drawing conclusions from factual evidence—is known as logic. Aristotle was the first philosopher to create a formal system of logic, in which he clearly outlined the procedures all thinkers should use when trying to understand the world around them. Today, logical thinking has become second nature. For example, if we look out the window on a winter day and see people wearing hats and scarves, we logically conclude that it is cold outside. Of course, this is just an assumption based on a piece of evidence. To prove that it really is cold outdoors, we would have to step outside ourselves (preferably with a thermometer) to test the air.

Using logical connections, such as the example below, to arrive at a conclusion is known as syllogism. A famous example of syllogism states:

1. All men are mortal (they are born, live, and die).
2. Socrates is a man.
3. Thus, the logical conclusion, based on deduction, is that Socrates is mortal.

By using logic, Aristotle also believed it was possible to organize the chaos of the world into ordered categories. For instance, he divided all matter on Earth into three groups: animal, vegetable, and mineral. Each main group could be broken down into subcategories based on similarities and differences.

An example of this was Aristotle's classification of animals into "bloodless" and "blooded," which were then further divided into other subcategories.

SCIENCE

At the Lyceum, while Aristotle continued to pursue his passion for classifying and studying animals, his friend Theophrastus turned his attention to the vegetable (plants) and mineral groups. In his book *Account of Plants*, Theophrastus succeeded in identifying and describing more than 550 plant species. He divided these into categories such as trees, shrubs, and herbs. This undertaking led Theophrastus to be considered the world's first botanist. Botany is the study of plant life.

Although his great passion was natural science, Aristotle brought new approaches to many other scientific fields. For example, he was the first to distinguish between mathematics and physics as two separate disciplines. Previously, ancient Greek scholars had used mathematics to explain natural occurrences ranging from the arrangement of the stars and planets in the sky to the notes created by musical instruments. Many had been inspired by the teachings of the great sixth-century-BC mathematician

Theophrastus is shown in this engraving wearing a traditional cloak—called a himation—that was worn by both women and men in ancient Greece. This was a piece of heavy fabric (usually linen or wool) that was draped over one shoulder and then attached at the other. Himations were especially popular with politicians and intellectuals. In fact, Plato was famous for stating that a gentleman should never let his arm protrude from his himation.

THEOPHRASTVS. 14.

Dulcius expreſſit te verbis nemo politis
Materias Medicûm, quidquid & orbis alit:
Inde tibi venit diuinum nomen ab ore,
Diſcipulus tanto dignus Ariſtotele es.

Pythagoras, who believed that the world could be reduced to numbers and formulas.

For Aristotle, however, mathematics was an abstract science that dealt with shapes, volumes, and calculations. In contrast, physics was a concrete science that explained how and why things functioned as they did and the reasons they changed. Aristotle wrote a series of essays on these questions that were grouped together and published under the title *Physics* (circa 350 BC).

Aristotle believed that all matter was capable of undergoing four kinds of changes. The first three were physical changes. However, when matter changed its very substance, this was a chemical

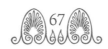

Type of Change	Example
1) Change in location (movement)	A rock pushed from a cliff into a lake
2) Change in quality (alteration)	Water that freezes and becomes ice
3) Change in size (expansion or contraction)	A piece of chewing gum that is stretched into a long ribbon
4) Change in substance	Melting together of tin and copper to make bronze

change. For instance, to make bronze, ancient Greeks melted together tin and copper. Once the mixture had solidified, it would no longer be possible to extract either of the original substances (tin or copper) from the new substance (bronze).

According to Aristotle, two elements were involved in any change: the substances that underwent an alteration and the forces responsible for causing the change. The forces were external. When applied to tin and copper, heat was the force that caused both

This is the preface of Aristotle's famous work *Physics*. Written in the fourth century BC, this book (broken down into eight books) was considered to be the authority on the subject throughout the Middle Ages and up until the sixteenth century. It was in the early 1600s that the famous Italian mathematician Galileo (1564–1642) refuted Aristotle's laws of motion and instead argued that the speed at which something falls is not dependent upon its weight.

metals to melt and mix together, becoming bronze. The changing of the seasons and the resulting differences in weather conditions (varying amounts of heat, cold, rain, and sunshine) caused the birth, growth, and death of all plant life.

In his book *Meteorology* (circa 350 BC), Aristotle attempted to explain the changes and forces that affected Earth. Modern-day meteorology refers to the study of weather, but for Aristotle, it embraced all natural occurrences on Earth ranging from thunder, lightning, winds, and earthquakes to ocean tides and tidal waves. Among his important discoveries was that the sun played a key role in Earth's hydraulic (or water) cycle. In *Meteorology*, Aristotle explained evaporation and precipitation, stating that "by its [the sun's] agency [actions] the finest and sweetest water is every day carried up and is dissolved into vapor and rises to the upper regions, where it is condensed again by the cold and so returns to the earth."

Aristotle encountered difficulty when it came to understanding astronomical phenomena such as stars, comets, and meteors. Since he could find no cause for the movement of these bodies, he had to assume that an "Unmoved Mover," or God, was responsible for these changes. The "Unmoved Mover" was an eternal force. Aristotle wrote about the idea of God in a group of essays called *Metaphysics* (circa 350 BC). *Meta* is the Greek work for "after." Fittingly, *Metaphysics* was the book that came after Aristotle's collection of essays entitled *Physics.*

Metaphysics's opening line would become one of Aristotle's most memorable declarations: "All men by nature have a desire for knowledge." Aristotle believed that it was our need to understand things and our ability to think rationally that set human beings apart from the rest of the animal kingdom and brought us closer to God.

ETHICS

Aside from science, Aristotle was interested in many other aspects of human existence. His series of essays on ethics (rules that state how to behave) outlined basic human codes of social conduct. Of his three books on ethics, the most famous is *Nicomachean Ethics* (circa 350 BC), which Aristotle wrote as a rule book for his young son, Nicomachus. Following ancient Greek tradition, Aristotle's son had been named in honor of Aristotle's father. He was born to Aristotle's second wife, Herpyllis, a woman from Stagira whom the philosopher had married following the death of his first wife, Pythias.

A page from Aristotle's *Nicomachean Ethics* provides a wonderful example of a text that was written using calligraphy. Although the printing press had been invented by Johannes Gutenberg in 1450, calligraphy as a writing style remained popular until the end of the fifteenth century. This is a modern English translation of the first line of the first chapter in book 1: "EVERY art and every inquiry, and similarly every action and pursuit, is thought to aim at some good; and for this reason the good has rightly been declared to be that at which all things aim."

est tale esse ut aliquid turpe faciat. Verū ita se hēt
ut si faciat gnicūy tale verecundetur, et propt'hoc
putare probū esse absurdū ē. Et n̄ verecundia ī
voluntarius est. Volens aut probus or mūy facit
prava. Esset aut verecundia ex suppositione
vtique probū. Si n̄ faciat verēdabit. Sed n̄ est
hoc circa vtutes. Impudentia vo improbū et n̄
verecundari m male agat. Sed mhtomagis hoc
faciente verecundari probū ē. Contiuētia quoque ver
ipa qnidē vtus ē. sed queda mixta. Ostendemus
aut de illa postea. Nunc de iusticia dicamus

Quintus ethicorum liber incipit

De Iusticia et iniusticia
consideradū est, et circa gnas res consistant et qualis
mediocritas iusticia sit, et iustū quoq medm. Consideratio
aut ista eode modo nobis sit. Ut ī precedentibus. Videmus

Videmus igitur omēs.

Aristotle declared that young people (whom he believed to be naturally undisciplined and filled with energy) required strict laws to teach them the difference between right and wrong. This kind of knowledge would help them become responsible citizens. Aristotle also believed that the highest goal in a person's life was the pursuit of happiness. People who sought riches and fame and believed that these things would make them happy were mistaken. Happiness, however, was not to be confused with pleasure. Instead, in *Nicomachean Ethics*, Aristotle defined happiness as "an activity of the soul according to goodness in a mature person."

Aristotle also placed a very high value on friendship. "Without friends no one would choose to live, though he had all other goods," he wrote in *Nicomachean Ethics*. Known for his lifelong friendships with many men, such as Theophrastus, it is clear that Aristotle practiced what he preached.

POLITICS

Aristotle lived during turbulent political times. As a friend and tutor of Alexander, he had firsthand experience of the workings of governments led by kings and tyrants. Living in democratic Athens allowed

Aristotle to observe the world's first citizens' government ruled by popular assembly. At the same time, he witnessed the constant threats to democracy. Aristotle analyzed the impacts these different forms of government had on human lives. Based on his observations, he constructed his ideas of an ideal society governed by an ideal form of government.

Having thrived as a teacher and intellectual under Athenian democracy, it was no surprise that Aristotle championed a democratic state in which all men were free and equal and allowed to participate in their own government. He also believed that a state, or nation, was not merely a community of people that banded together for defensive and commercial reasons, but rather a society whose goal should be "noble actions." By this, he meant that individuals had a duty to work together in order to create a better, more harmonious society.

POETICS

Theater played an enormous role in Greek life. In ancient Athens, theaters themselves were important public monuments, and playwrights were highly respected members of society. Great playwrights such as Sophocles (circa 496 BC–406 BC) and Euripides

Famous Greek playwright Euripides is shown here on this relief sculpture dating from the imperial Roman period, 2 BC. The writer is seated in front of a wall containing an unfinished alphabetical listing of the titles of all of his plays. Known as the stage philosopher, Euripides was instrumental in spreading an awareness and respect for dramatic literature. It was said that his plays were among the most tragic of his contemporaries.

(circa 484 BC–406 BC) often inserted philosophical arguments into the text of their comedies and tragedies. Aside from becoming emotionally engaged, the public was meant to reflect upon the serious issues addressed in a play.

In *Poetics*, Aristotle developed very precise theories about theater, specifically tragedy. He felt that a proper tragedy was made up of six key elements: plot, character, diction (speech), thought, spectacle, and song. The plot should be about one important action. Unlike comedies, which were meant to have happy endings, a tragedy traced the downfall of the main character. The downfall was usually brought

Imitation of Life

Both Aristotle and Plato viewed art as a mimesis (the origin of the English words "mime" and "mimic") or imitation, of nature. However, Plato believed that this imitation was negative. For example, a painting of a bed could never provide a substitute for an actual bed. As such, art was seen as inferior—merely a cheap imitation that was neither useful nor informative. Unsurprisingly, in Plato's famous work *The Republic*, in which he outlined his ideal society, artists possessed no useful function. Plato even suggested that they be banished. He believed that artists were dangerous to society because they relied on lies and illusions and provoked emotions that interfered with people's rational thoughts.

In contrast, Aristotle viewed mimesis as being positive. In one of his most renowned works, *Poetics* (circa 350 BC), he wrote that art completes what nature cannot finish. By this he meant that, for example, a painting of a bed represented more than a simple object. Depending on the artist's imagination and skill, this representation could bring about new types and uses of beds. In this sense, art wasn't simply reproducing something that already existed but rather reinventing other potential realities. As such, the artist became a useful member of society whose work resulted in new inventions and ways of thinking. Aristotle also viewed people's emotional reactions to works of art as something positive. He claimed that a person's pleasure in art was equal to the pleasure felt in learning something new about the world.

Pictured above are the archaeological ruins of the famous Greek theater in Taormina, Sicily. Greek theaters were large, open-air structures that were most often built on hillsides in order to provide for natural terraced (or sloped) seating. That way, no matter where one sat, the view to the flat performance area would be clear. It is believed that the first of such theaters to be built in Europe was the Dionysus Theater in Athens. Dionysus was the god of wine and theater.

about by a serious flaw or weakness (such as stubbornness or excessive pride) in the heroic character.

Since Aristotle thought the most important human goal was the pursuit of happiness, how could he justify the value of a tragedy that made people feel sad or despairing? He reasoned that in watching the downfall of a noble character, audience members were able to relieve themselves of feelings of fear and pity. In

other words, after viewing a tragic play, spectators felt a positive sensation of relief. Aristotle called this sensation a "catharsis."

Originally, "catharsis" was a medical term that referred to purging (getting rid of) dangerous elements in a person's body that were causing illness. Aristotle felt that if everyone in the audience watching a play experienced a catharsis, this would result in a common bond that would reinforce a sense of community.

In *Poetics*, Aristotle also discussed two other important types of writing: poetry and history. He

This sketch show's a messenger's costume in Euripides' tragic play *Hippolytus* (428 BC). The play also featured a singing chorus, the Greek goddess of love and beauty, Aphrodite, and Hippolytus (the son of Theseus)—among others. About the origins of dramatic theater, Aristotle said, "Some say that dramas are so called, because their authors represent the characters as "doing" them (*drôntes*). And it is on this basis that the Dorians [the Spartans, etc.] lay claim to the invention of both tragedy and comedy."

reasoned that the difference between the two was more than the obvious fact that one was written in verse and the other in prose. Aristotle pointed out that while history deals with facts from the past, poetry concerns itself with imagining the possibilities of the future. He concluded that poetry was a superior art since it deals with universal human issues, while history simply relates details of events that have already taken place.

5 | THE PHILOSOPHER

In Athens, Aristotle (who was considered by many of his contemporaries as the greatest thinker known to mankind) was revolutionizing how people understood the world. Meanwhile, his former pupil, Alexander, was changing the map of the world. By the age of thirty, Alexander had conquered much of the lands known to human beings. At one time or another, he was emperor of Greece, king of Persia, pharaoh of Egypt, and ruler of Asia. His bravery earned him the title of the world's greatest warrior. Subsequently, he would be known throughout history as Alexander the Great.

THE END OF ALEXANDER

Over time, however, Alexander began to believe in the myths of his own greatness.

Though Alexander the Great had conquered a huge empire in a short period of time—thirteen years—even he could not outlive life itself. This page from a Persian manuscript illustrates Alexander (or Ishkandar, as he was called by the Persians) being told that ultimately, even he would be conquered by death. He died of a fever in a palace in Babylon at the young age of thirty-two. Because he was such a magnificent leader, historians often speculate as to whether or not he did, in fact, die of natural causes.

As he became more and more obsessed with his own power, he became increasingly angry with anyone who dared to challenge him. A close friend, Cleitus (who had once saved his life), criticized him for defying convention by dressing in Persian clothing. Alexander was so furious that he plunged a spear into Cleitus's heart, killing him instantly. Another time, he was so offended when Aristotle's nephew, Callisthenes, disagreed with him, that he forced him into an iron cage. For days, Callisthenes was carried around in this cage while maggots, fleas, and lice attacked him. He was then put to a horrible death when he was fed to a hungry lion.

When news of Callisthenes reached Aristotle, the philosopher was shocked. Relations between Aristotle and Alexander were severed, and they never reconnected. Meanwhile, Alexander continued his conquest of the world, even though, by this time, many of his formerly loyal followers feared and even hated him. In 326 BC, after sweeping through Afghanistan and Pakistan, he arrived at the borders of India.

Here, he met his match against India's King Porous, whose fierce army attacked Alexander's troops. Although he succeeded in capturing King Porous, Alexander's much-loved companion, Bucephalus, was killed in battle. Overcome with grief, Alexander lost his will to fight. Meanwhile, his men refused to advance any further, believing that they had already reached the end of the world. Hence, after setting the Indian king free and founding a city—named Bucephala (present-day Jhelum in Pakistan) in honor of his faithful horse—Alexander began leading his exhausted troops back to Greece. Weakened and weary, he never completed the long trip home. After coming down with a severe fever (probably malaria), he died in Babylon, in 323 BC.

Alexander didn't have any children or heirs, so there was no one to take his place as ruler of an enormous empire. Without a strong central power, fighting broke out between the leaders of various territories. The empire soon began to fall apart. Nonetheless, Alexander's conquests had permanently changed the map. The thousands of Macedonians and Greeks who had traveled with him on his campaign settled in the new cities he had founded in places as far-flung as Egypt, Syria, and Persia. As a result, Greek culture took root and had a long-lasting impact in these lands.

THE END OF ARISTOTLE

When news of Alexander's death reached Athens, most Athenians were happy. They had resented the

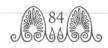

Macedonian conquest of their formerly independent city. With hostilities on the rise, many Macedonians decided to leave the city. Aristotle was very well respected in Athens. However, his relationship with Alexander, as well as the generous contributions Alexander had made to the Lyceum were public knowledge. As a result, some important Athenians doubted his loyalty. Because Aristotle was so famous, he became an easy target for anti-Macedonian sentiment.

It wasn't long before the same charges that had been brought against Socrates were being leveled at Aristotle. Remembering the fate of Socrates, Aristotle vowed that he wouldn't give the Athenians another chance to, as he put it, "sin against philosophy." Instead of waiting for his trial, he fled Athens with his wife and two children and escaped to Euboea. In the town of Chalcis, he and his family settled in the house that had once belonged to his mother. Less than a year after going into exile, Aristotle became ill with stomach pains and a fever. He died in 322 BC at the age of sixty-two.

When Aristotle departed from Athens, he had left the Lyceum in the care of Theophrastus. He had also left him in charge of his personal library, which included all his lecture notes, books, and research.

This portrait depicts Aristotle later in life. After Aristotle died, his philosophical thoughts continued to be taught. One of his successors, a philosopher named Critolaus, passed on Aristotle's ideas to Rome as a result of his travels there in 155 BC. This was the first time Romans had contact with ancient Greek thought. Around 100 years later, his works were translated, thus reawakening interest in his philosophy.

ARISTOTLE'S WRITINGS

When Theophrastus died in 287 BC, he left Aristotle's library to his nephew, Neleus, who lived in the town of Skepsis, in Asia Minor. After Neleus's death, what happened to Aristotle's writings is somewhat of a mystery. According to some historians, Neleus's relatives sold many of his manuscripts to the great library at Alexandria. They hid other texts in a cave. Two centuries later, a book collector named Apellico was traveling through Skepsis and heard tales about these buried manuscripts. After uncovering them, he took them back to his own private library in Athens.

In 84 BC, a Roman general named Sulla led an invasion of Athens. Once the city was under Roman control, Sulla seized Apellico's precious collection and took them to a library in Rome. They were forgotten for years until they came to the attention of Cicero, a famous Roman writer and politician. He recognized they were the works of a great philosopher. Cicero praised Aristotle's ideas and quoted him extensively in his own writings, which were widely read and respected in Rome. As such, Aristotle's teachings were diffused throughout the Roman Empire.

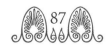

Shortly after, around 30 BC, a scholar named Andronicus from the Greek island of Rhodes decided to edit all of Aristotle's surviving works. All in all, according to Aristotle's first biographer, Diogenes Laertius (circa AD 200–300), the philosopher had written more than 150 titles. Most of these, however, had been handwritten on scrolls made of fragile parchment paper. Unfortunately, many were lost or damaged over time. In fact, none of the books Aristotle wrote while he was at the Academy survived. Luckily, these manuscripts were read by other scholars, who copied down or quoted portions of the originals in their own works. The majority of Aristotle's surviving texts consisted of the lecture notes he wrote during his years in Assos, in Pella, and at the Lyceum.

For a long time, Aristotle's theories were much less influential than those of his master, Plato. In fact, after the fall of the Roman Empire in AD 476, his works were scarcely read in Europe. However, in the Middle East, Arab scholars highly valued his teachings. When Arabs invaded Europe in the twelfth and thirteenth centuries, Aristotle was rediscovered in Europe. His works were translated into Latin, the major written language in Europe at the time. His theories became incredibly influential as well. While many of Plato's teachings lost favor with European scholars, Aristotle came to be considered the greatest philosopher of all time.

THE IMPORTANCE OF QUESTIONING

In fact, during the Middle Ages, the title of "the Philosopher" was given to Aristotle by Scholastic thinkers who mixed his philosophy with Christian beliefs. His theories were embraced by the Catholic Church, which had become increasingly popular. As a result, Aristotle's views were considered to be sacred. In fact, his writings carried the same authority as the Bible. Even observations of his that were quite incorrect could not be questioned by other scholars or philosophers. To criticize Aristotle's beliefs was considered a sin. This was quite ironic since Aristotle firmly believed in the importance of challenging authority. For him, questioning established facts was an essential means of discovering new knowledge.

Today, many scholars believe that this absolute belief in Aristotle's theories hindered scientific progress in the West for centuries. In fact, until the scientific revolution of the sixteenth and seventeenth centuries, scientists risked their lives whenever they publicly proposed theories that conflicted with Aristotle's.

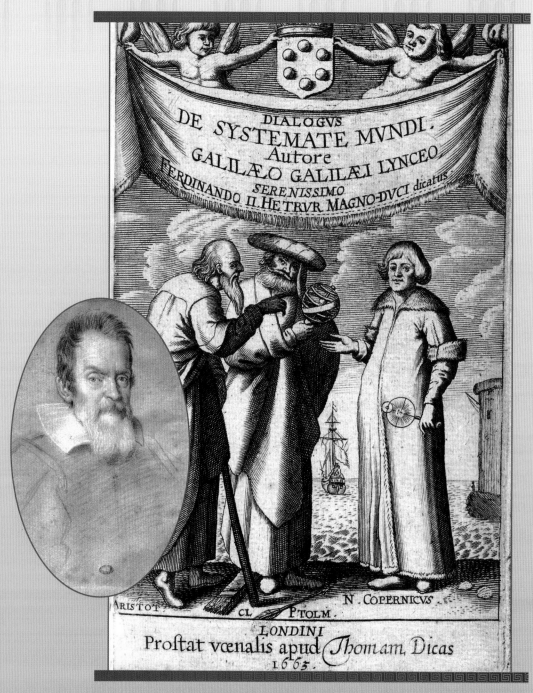

A portrait of famous Italian astronomer and physicist Galileo Galilei (*inset*). Featured above is the opening illustration (or frontispiece) titled "Cosmic System" by Galileo. Published in 1663, this illustration from an edition of Galileo's *Systema Cosmicum* (Cosmic System) shows Aristotle, Ptolemy, and Polish astronomer Nicolaus Copernicus. Aside from his work challenging Aristotle, Galileo is known for discovering the moons of the planet Jupiter.

CHALLENGES TO ARISTOTLE

One of the first major challenges to Aristotelian ideas came from the great Italian astronomer and physicist Galileo Galilei (1564–1642). Among the pioneers of modern science, Galileo used the scientific method of experimentation to solve problems. Unlike Aristotle, Galileo believed one couldn't reach a conclusion simply by using reason and logic. It was necessary to prove a conclusion by means of actual experimentation. Aristotle claimed that observing a thing made it real. Galileo countered that a thing could only be considered real if it had been measured and quantified.

Galileo did just this when he dropped two different-sized cannonballs from the Leaning Tower of Pisa and discovered that objects of different masses fall at the same speed. Aristotle had said quite the contrary. Based on logic, he believed that if one dropped two balls, and one was twice as heavy as the other, the heavier ball would fall twice as fast as the lighter ball. However, Aristotle had never backed up his theory by providing actual evidence. Had he performed such an experiment, he would have easily seen that his theory was wrong. Both balls would have hit the ground at almost the same time.

Galileo got into trouble for challenging another one of Aristotle's "truths"—that of a geocentric universe (*geo* is Greek for "earth"). According to this theory, Earth was the center of the world around which all other planets revolved. Galileo echoed the views of Polish astronomer Nicolaus Copernicus (1473–1543), who had proposed a heliocentric universe with planets, including Earth, revolving around the sun (*helio* is the Greek word for "sun").

Both men reached their conclusions with the aid of the newly invented telescope. Nonetheless, their theories were viewed as criminal in the eyes of the Catholic Church. The church firmly believed in Aristotle's statement that Earth is the center of the universe. After bringing Galileo to trial, the church forced him to reject his own beliefs of a sun-centered universe and then sentenced him to life imprisonment.

The belief in such inaccurate theories led many scholars in the seventeenth and eighteenth centuries to regard Aristotle as a deeply flawed scientist. Many scientists rejected Aristotle's beliefs in favor of exploring new theories and methods.

Flawed Conclusions

Over time, scientists discovered that some of Aristotle's theories about animals were flawed. Without the aid of sophisticated scientific equipment such as microscopes, Aristotle sometimes arrived at incorrect conclusions. For example, because he couldn't see their tiny eggs, he thought that some insects had no parents and emerged as full-grown adults from decomposing plants and the bodies of other animals. He was confused about whether dolphins breathed water or air. And he believed that honeybees flying in strong winds carried stones in order to balance their flight. Overall, however, his knowledge of the animal world was quite accurate.

Charles Darwin is most famous for his theories of evolution. His most cited work, *On the Origin of Species by Means of Natural Selection, or the Preservation of Favoured Races in the Struggle for Life*, presented an often quoted argument, which has become a catchphrase—"the survival of the fittest."

ARISTOTLE REDISCOVERED

Although many of Aristotle's theories about physics were eventually rejected, in the late nineteenth century, his observations concerning the natural sciences were rediscovered and applauded by biologists and zoologists. A great admirer of Aristotle's was the famous naturalist Charles Darwin, whose landmark book *On the Origin of Species* (1859) elaborated the theory of the evolution of species.

Darwin was impressed by Aristotle's thorough classification and descriptions of animals. He was also amazed at how much common knowledge had been based on Aristotle's premises. Indeed, some of Aristotle's more abstract ideas contained in *Ethics, Politics*, and *Poetics* (in which he examines timeless human issues such as pleasure, honor, art, justice, and democracy) are still very influential today.

CONCLUSION

Perhaps more than any other ancient philosopher, Aristotle's ideas have had a lasting impact on society. In fact, contemporary Western thought is often defined by philosophers as "Aristotelian." This is because it has become second nature for people to

This is an illuminated manuscript page from a fifteenth-century French translation of one of Aristotle's philosophical tracts. Aristotle's approach to ethics is teleological, meaning that he is less concerned with moral absolutes than he is with what is beneficial to the good of humans.

Words of Wisdom

Although many of Aristotle's surviving texts were unpolished lecture notes, he was known to have been an accomplished teacher, with a flair for rhetoric. To this day, many of his wise observations and reflections are frequently quoted. Here are some of the best known:

On humans:

"We are what we repeatedly do."

"All men by nature desire knowledge."

On nature:

"In all things of nature there is something of the marvelous."

"Nature does nothing uselessly."

On education:

"Education is the best provision for old age."

"It is the mark of an educated mind to be able to entertain a thought without accepting it."

On honesty:

"Liars when they speak the truth are not believed."

On poverty:

"Poverty is the parent of revolution and crime."

On war:

"We make war that we may live in peace."

On law:

"Law is order, and good law is good order."

On democracy:

"The only stable state is the one in which all men are equal before the law."

"The basis of a democratic state is liberty."

"If liberty and equality, as is thought by some, are chiefly to be found in democracy, they will be best attained when all persons alike share in government to the utmost."

On work:

"Pleasure in the job puts perfection in the work."

On friendship:

"Without friends no one would choose to live, though he had all other goods."

"Misfortune shows those who are not really friends."

"What is a friend? A single soul dwelling in two bodies."

think of the world around them in terms of facts and scientific categories.

When people don't understand something, they automatically search for reasonable and logical explanations based on physical evidence. They make lists and collect information. They try to classify things to give order and meaning to their lives. They rely on their senses—hearing, touch, smell, taste, and sight—to understand the external world. When they have a problem, they try to use reason to find a solution. All of these methods are so natural to people that this type of thinking is referred to as common sense. Ultimately, in some ways, common sense wouldn't exist if it hadn't been for Aristotle.

Although over time some of Aristotle's suppositions have been proven incorrect, many of his thoughts and ideas are as influential now as they were 2,000 years ago. Many of his theories concerning art, justice, education, and friendship have become guiding human principles.

Reading some of Aristotle's quotes reveals how influential his ideas have been in Western societies. In terms of the United States, his thoughts on democracy, equality, liberty, and justice inspired some of the founding principles of the American nation. They are echoed in the Constitution and the Bill of Rights,

and are often repeated by presidents and politicians. Even his thoughts on war—that it is necessary so "that we may live in peace"—were used in an argument made by the Bush administration for going to war against Iraq in 2003.

Whether one agrees with Aristotle or not, there is no denying the enormous impact he has left on modern thought. If people value education, have learned to question authority, and believe in reason, democracy, and the pursuit of happiness as an ultimate goal, it is because of his teachings. As one of the greatest philosophers of all time, Aristotle's philosophy continues to inform and inspire present and future generations of eager minds.

Timeline

384 BC   Aristotle is born at Stagira, a Greek colony in northern Greece, near the kingdom of Macedonia.

374 BC   Aristotle's father, Nicomachus, dies. A close family friend, Proxenus, becomes his guardian.

367 BC   At age seventeen, Aristotle is sent to Athens to study at Plato's Academy.

347 BC   Plato dies. Aristotle leaves Athens. He travels to Asia Minor (now Turkey) and settles at the court of King Hermias. He marries Hermias's niece, Pythias. Shortly after, she gives birth to a daughter, also named Pythias.

344 BC   Hermias is murdered, and Aristotle and his family move to Lesbos, where he begins his studies of land and sea creatures.

343 BC   Aristotle is invited to Macedonia to tutor Alexander, teenage son of Philip II, king of Macedonia.

338 BC   Philip takes control of all Greece, including Athens.

336 BC   Philip II is murdered, and Alexander becomes king of Macedonia and sets off to conquer the known world.

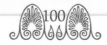

335 BC	Aristotle returns to Athens and creates his own school, the Lyceum. Here, he lectures, founds a museum and a library, and writes many of his famous works.
323 BC	Alexander the Great dies and the fall of his empire begins. There are revolts against Macedonians in Athens. Charged with "impiety," Aristotle flees Athens and settles in Chalcis on the island of Euboea.
322 BC	Aristotle dies on Euboea at the age of sixty-two, after complaining of a stomach illness. He leaves behind his second wife, Herpyllis; Nicomachus, the son they had together; and his daughter, Pythias.

GLOSSARY

articulate To express oneself powerfully, using clear, precise language.

assembly A public gathering where citizens discuss and vote upon laws for governing a city or state.

assumption Something taken for granted or accepted as true without proof.

authoritarian Relating to absolute and strict obedience.

banished To be expelled.

city-state A city that exists as an individual state or country.

constitutional government A government whose laws are based on the codes and rules set out in a nation's written constitution.

deteriorate To fall or crumble apart.

diction A careful, correct speaking style with an emphasis on clear choice of words.

epic Something heroic and impressive that celebrates a legendary moment or event; can refer specifically to a long narrative poem written in a grand style with a heroic theme.

ethics A set of rules of good conduct; a system of moral values.

exiled To be forced from one's country.

freethinking Rejecting established or official theories in favor of new ideas based on rational investigation.

fresco A style of painting that involves applying paint to wet plaster.

hemlock A deadly liquid poison derived from the hemlock plant.

legacy Something handed down from a predecessor or ancestor.

malaria An infectious and often deadly disease spread by mosquitoes in tropical climates.

matter A physical substance that occupies space and can be perceived by the senses.

mentor A wise and trusted teacher or counselor.

mock To make fun of.

monarchy A nation ruled by a king or queen.

objective Having to do with a real, material object that can be perceived.

orator A skilled public speaker.

physician A medical doctor or healer.

prophetic Predicting events to come.

rational Based on reason or logic.

recoil To jump back or shrink away from.

Scholastic thinkers Dominant school of philosophers in Europe during the Middle Ages who adhered to Aristotle's theories and Christian beliefs.

scorned Unwanted; unworthy; undesirable.

subjective Having to do with an idea imagined by an individual; something that comes from a person's mind instead of from the real, material world.

tyrant An absolute ruler who governs without limits.

upheaval A violent disruption or upsetting event.

FOR MORE INFORMATION

The Ancient Philosophy Society
4554 Mayflower Hill
Colby College
Waterville, ME 04901
(207) 872-3140
Web site: http://www.trincoll.edu/orgs/aps/
    contact.htm

The Aristotelian Society
Room 260 Senate House
Malet Street
London, England WC1E 7HU
(44) 020 7255 1724
Web site: http://www.sas.ac.uk/aristotelian_society

The Center for Hellenic Studies
3100 Whitehaven Street NW
Washington, DC 20008
(202) 745-4400
Web site: http://www.chs.harvard.edu

The Metropolitan Museum of Art
Greek and Roman Art Department
1000 Fifth Avenue at 82nd Street
New York, NY 10028
(212) 535-7710
Web site: http://www.metmuseum.org/Works_Of_Art/
    department.asp?dep=13

Society for Ancient Greek Philosophy
Binghamton University
Binghamton, NY 13902-6000
(607) 777-2886
Web site: http://sagp.binghamton.edu

WEB SITES

Due to the changing nature of Internet links, the
Rosen Publishing Group, Inc., has developed an
online list of Web sites related to the subject of
this book. This site is updated regularly. Please
use this link to access the list:

http://www.rosenlinks.com/lgp/aris

FOR FURTHER READING

Anderson, Margaret, and Karen Stephenson. *Aristotle: Philosopher and Scientist*. Berkeley Heights, NJ: Enslow Publishers, 2004.

Code, Alan D. *Aristotle*. Boulder, CO: Westview Press, 2003.

Hakim, Joy. *The Story of Science: Aristotle Leads the Way*. Washington, DC: Smithsonian Books, 2004.

Sedley, David. *The Cambridge Companion to Greek and Roman Philosophy*. New York, NY: Cambridge University Press, 2003.

Williams, Brian. *Aristotle*. Chicago, IL: Heinemann Library, 2002.

Woodfin, Rupert. *Introducing Aristotle*. New York, NY: Totem Books, 2001.

BIBLIOGRAPHY

Anderson, Margaret, and Karen Stephenson. *Aristotle: Philosopher and Scientist*. Berkeley Heights, NJ: Enslow Publishers, 2004.

BBC.co.uk. "Athens." Retrieved January 2005 (http://www.bbc.co.uk/ schools/ancientgreece/ athens/index.shtml).

History for Kids. "Aristotle." Retrieved January 2005 (http://www.historyforkids.org/learn/greeks/ philosophy/aristotle.htm).

Kids' Philosophy Slam Page. "Aristotle." Retrieved January 2005 (http://www.philosophyslam.org/ aristotle.html).

PBS.org. "The Greeks Crucible of Civilization." Retrieved January 2005 (http://www.pbs.org/ empires/thegreeks/htmlver/).

Professor Fred L. Wilson's Web Page. Rochester Institute of Technology. "Science and Human Values: Aristotle." Retrieved January 2005 (http://www.rit.edu/~flwstv/ aristotle1.html).

A Progressive Living Biography. "Aristotle." Retrieved January 2005 (http://progressiveliving.org/ aristotle_biography.htm).

Stanford Encyclopedia of Philosophy. "Aristotle's Ethics," "Aristotle's Logic," "Aristotle's Meta-physics," "Aristotle's Political Theory," "Aristotle's Rhetoric." Retrieved February 2005 (http://plato. stanford.edu/contents.html#a, http://plato. stanford.edu/entries/aristotle-ethics, http://plato. stanford.edu/entries/aristotle-logic, http://plato. stanford.edu/entries/aristotle-politics, http:// plato.stanford.edu/entries/aristotle-metaphysics, http://plato.stanford.edu/entries/aristotle-rhetoric).

University of California, Berkeley Museum of Paleontology, Aristotle page. Retrieved January 2005 (http://www.ucmp.berkeley.edu/history/ aristotle.html).

Wikipedia. "Aristotle." Retrieved January 2005 (http://en.wikipedia.org/wiki/Aristotle).

INDEX

ABOUT THE AUTHOR

Mick Isle has been writing books for Rosen for more than half a decade. Since acquiring a degree in journalism from Trinity College in Dublin, Ireland—where he also took many courses in philosophy and ancient Greek civilization—Mick has worked consistently as a freelance journalist, both in his native Ireland and in the United States.

PHOTO CREDITS

Cover, title page, pp. 42–43 Vatican Museums and Galleries, Vatican City, Italy, Giraudon/Bridgeman Art Library; cover (inset), title page (inset), pp. 69, 86 Scala/Art Resource, NY; p. 7 © Corbis; p. 9 Ethica Nicomachea, Politica, Economica, Rare Book and Manuscript Library, Columbia University; pp. 14–15 Originally published in Historical Atlas of the World, © J. W. Cappelens Forlag A/S, Oslo, 1962. Maps by Berit Lie. Used with permission of J. W. Cappelens Forlag; pp. 18–19 © The British Library/Topham-HIP/The Image Works; p. 20 Museé d'Orsay, Paris, France, Giraudon/Bridgeman Art Library; p. 22 Peter Connolly/ akg-images; p. 23 © Royalty-Free/Corbis; pp. 28, 51, 79 Erich Lessing/ Art Resource, NY; p. 32 Private Collection, Charles Plante Fine Arts/ Bridgeman Art Library; pp. 35, 63 akg-images; p. 36 The Art Archive/ Bodleian Library Oxford/The Bodleian Library; p.39 © Alinari Archives/ Corbis; p. 45 Bibliotheque Mazarine, Paris, France, Archives Charmet/ Bridgeman Art library; p. 53 © The British Library/Topham/The Image Works; p. 55 Museé de la Ville de Paris, Museé du Petie-Palais, France, Lauros/Giraudon/Bridgeman Art Library; p.58 Museé de Vulliod Saint-Germain, Pezenas, France, Giraudon/Bridgeman Art Library; p. 61 © AP/Wide World Photos; p. 67 Private Collection, Archives Charmet/ Bridgeman Art library; pp. 72–73 The Remnant Trust, Inc., Hagerstown, Indiana, www.theremnanttrust.com; p. 76 Réunion des Musées Nationaux/Art Resource, NY; p. 78 © Piotr Malecki/Getty Images; p. 82 Bodleian Library, Oxford © Ann Ronan Picture Library/HIP/The Image Works; p. 90 © SSPL/The Image Works; p. 90 inset Biblioteca Marucelliana, Florence, Italy, Alinari/Bridgeman Art Library; p. 93 © NMPFT/Kodak Collection/SSPL/The Image Works; p. 95 Bibliotheque Municipale, Rouen, France, Lauros/Giraudon/Bridgeman Art Library.

Designer: Tahara Anderson

Editor: Annie Sommers

Photo Researcher: Amy Feinberg